J
917.1
~~L986~~
LYE, KEITH
Take a trip to Canada

JAN   1985

8.40

DATE DUE

TP YP	JUN 28 '95	
JUN 2 4 1985	APR 23 1997	
JUL 0 5 1985	OCT 1 5 1997	
SEP 0 9 1985	JAN 0 6 2000	
JAN 2 2 1987		
MAR 1 4 1990		
FEB 20 '91		
MAY 15 '93		
JUN 29 '93		
MAR 1 2 '94		

843600

Withdrawn

**PARK COUNTY LIBRARY
SYSTEM
CENTRAL LIBRARY**
Cody, Wyoming 82414

T2-BZO-380

CANADA

Keith Lye

General Editor

Henry Pluckrose

843600

Franklin Watts

London   New York   Sydney   Toronto

Facts about Canada

Area:
9,976,139 sq. km.
(3,852,019 sq. miles)
Canada is larger than
the USA

Population:
23,941,000 (1980)

Capital:
Ottawa

Largest cities:
Toronto (2,803,000);
Montreal (2,802,000);
Vancouver (1,166,000);
Ottawa (693,000);
Winnipeg (578,000)

Official languages:
English, French

Main religion:
Christianity

Major exports:
Motor cars, newsprint
and wood pulp, oil and
natural gas, wheat,
machinery

Currency:
Dollar

Franklin Watts Limited
12a Golden Square
London W1

ISBN: UK Edition 0 86313 041 0
ISBN: US Edition 0 531 03757 6
Library of Congress Catalog Card No:
83-60901

© Franklin Watts Limited 1983

Reprinted 1984

Typeset by Ace Filmsetting Ltd,
Frome, Somerset
Printed in Hong Kong

Text Editor: Brenda Williams
Maps: Tony Payne
Design: Peter Benoist
Photographs: Zefa; Canadian Tourist
Office, London, 26; Canadian National
Railways, 30; Province of British
Columbia, 16, 25, 29; Government of
Alberta, 20, 23, 28; Government of
Saskatchewan, 24; Ontario House,
London, 19, 31
Front Cover: Zefa
Back Cover: Province of British
Columbia

Canada is the world's second largest
country. Only Russia is bigger. But
Canada has few people for its size.
There are only a few big cities and
hardly anyone lives in the large areas
of forests, lakes and mountains. Most
Canadians live in the south, for the
north is bitterly cold.

The Blackfoot Indians once hunted buffalo on the plains of central Canada. The Indians were North America's first people. Their ancestors came from Asia over 20,000 years ago.

4

The ancestors of the Eskimos also came from Asia. Their way of life was suited to the cold of northern Canada. Canadian Eskimos are called Inuit. Many fish with modern tools and drive snowmobiles.

A former province of France, Canada became a British colony in 1763. Ottawa is in the Province of Ontario and is Canada's capital city. It has both French- and English-speaking people.

Most people in the Province of Quebec speak French. Out of every 100 Canadians, 29 have French ancestors and 45 have British ancestors. There are also people from many other parts of Europe.

This picture shows some stamps and money used in Canada. The main unit of currency is the dollar, which is divided into 100 cents.

Canada

ARCTIC OCEAN

GREENLAND

Ellesmere
Island

ALASKA

Beaufort
Sea

Davis Strait

Victoria
Island

Baffin Island

Yukon

Mackenzie R

Northwest Territories

Great
Bear Lake

PACIFIC OCEAN

Rocky Mountains

Great Slave
Lake

CANADA

Hudson
Bay

Labrador

Coastal Mts

Edmonton

Newfoundland

Vancouver

Calgary

Saskatoon

L. Winnipeg

St. John's

Regina

St Lawrence

Winnipeg

Quebec

Nova Scotia

Halifax

Great
Lakes

Montreal

Ottawa

Toronto

UNITED STATES
OF AMERICA

Hamilton

ATLANTIC OCEAN

9

Canada's parliament in Ottawa has both a House of Commons and a Senate. The country is divided into ten provinces and two territories. Each province has its own government. Canada became independent in 1931, but the British Queen is still Canada's Head of State.

The Royal Canadian Mounted Police give exciting displays of horsemanship. The red-coated "Mounties" were once famous for tracking criminals on horseback. They now use modern forms of transport to do their police work.

Toronto is the capital of the Province of Ontario and a major business city. The Canadian National Tower behind the skyscrapers is the world's largest self-supporting structure.

Visitors to Montreal can tour the old town in horse-drawn carriages. Montreal is a large city in Quebec. It stands on the St Lawrence River, Canada's most important waterway. This great city was founded by the French in 1642. Most of its people speak French.

Vancouver is in the Province of British Columbia, in the far west of Canada. Founded in 1884, it is Canada's third largest city and the country's most important port on the Pacific Ocean.

Polar bears hunt for fish, seals and young walruses around the ice floes of northern Canada. Few people live in these cold Arctic regions. In fact, nearly four-fifths of the country is almost uninhabited.

Forests cover about a third of Canada. Logging is a major industry. Much of the wood is made into pulp for producing paper. Canada leads the world in pulp and paper production.

Rodeos such as the Calgary Stampede are reminders of the early days of the Canadian west. Calgary is in the Province of Alberta, on the eastern side of the Rocky Mountains. Here cattle ranching is still important.

The Rocky Mountains are in western Canada. They reach 3,954 metres (12,972 feet) at Mount Robson. But Mount Logan is Canada's highest peak. It reaches 6,050 metres (19,849 feet) in the north-western St Elias Mountains.

The Niagara Falls on the Niagara River are made up of two parts. The Horseshoe Falls are in Canada, while the American Falls are in the USA. The Niagara River links Lakes Erie and Ontario, which are two of North America's Great Lakes.

Family life in Canada is much like
that in other western countries.
People enjoy various kinds of food,
including British, French and other
European dishes. Fast foods such as
hamburgers are also very popular
as they can be prepared quickly.

Many Canadian children go to nursery schools and kindergartens. Between the ages of 6 and 16 they must attend school. In elementary schools there are seven or eight grades (year-groups). Secondary or high schools have four or five grades.

843600

Even in southern Canada, heavy
snow is common in winter. Ice-
skating, riding on sleds and skiing
are popular pastimes. At home, most
of the family take turns to clear snow
from the driveway.

22

Ice hockey teams play before large crowds throughout Canada. Baseball and Canadian football, which is very like American football, golf, skating, curling and tennis are other leading sports.

Wheat is the major crop in Canada. Most of it grows on the treeless plains of the Prairie Provinces of Alberta, Saskatchewan and Manitoba. Only 5 per cent of Canada is farmed, and only 4 per cent of its people work on farms. But Canada is one of the world's top producers of cereals.

The Okanagan Valley in British Columbia is famous for its apples. This sheltered valley has little rain. But the fruit farmers irrigate their orchards with water taken from Lake Okanagan.

Fishing is important in Canada. Newfoundland, the easternmost of Canada's provinces, was visited by an English expedition in 1497. Soon afterwards, sailors from the British Isles began fishing around Newfoundland's coast.

This open-cast mine in Canada produces asbestos. Canada is among the world's top six producers of asbestos, gold, iron ore, lead, natural gas, nickel, potash, silver, uranium and zinc. It also has oil wells.

Canada's main oilfields and petro-chemical plants are in Alberta. Oil is also piped from Alberta to other refineries in Canada and the USA. Canada is the world's tenth largest oil producer. But the country now earns most of its money from manufactured goods.

Waneta Dam is in southern British Columbia. Dams are built across many rivers and at some there are hydroelectric plants. About 70 per cent of Canada's electricity is produced by such plants. Their electricity supplies power to homes and factories.

Canada's railways cross the country and span North America from the east to the west. In places, the trains wind along scenic mountain tracks. The first east–west railway was completed in 1885. Highways and airlines also serve the cities.

The St Lawrence Seaway was
made from parts of the St Lawrence
River, linked by canals. It leads from
the Atlantic Ocean to the Great
Lakes. Ocean-going ships use it to
call at industrial cities on the river
and lakes. Completed in 1958, the
Seaway showed that Canada had
become a major industrial power.

Index